T0132240

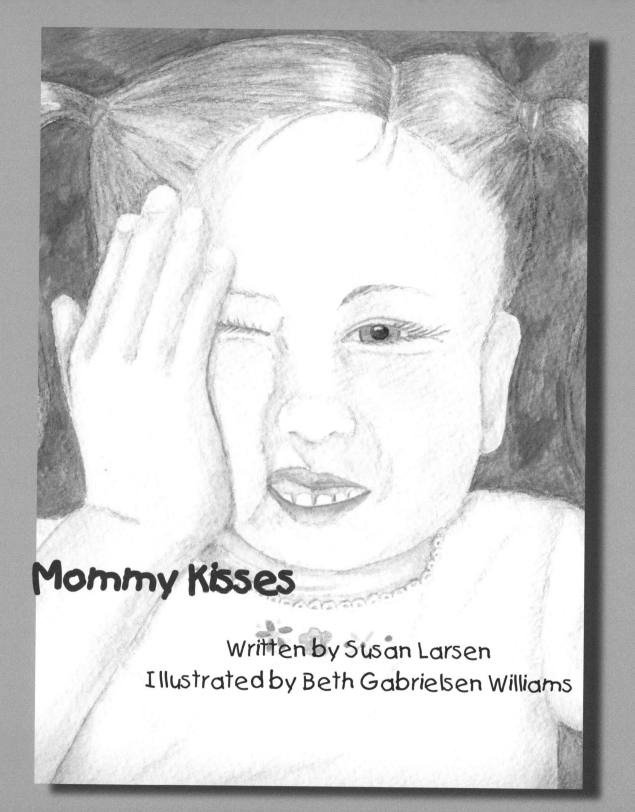

Mommy Kisses

Written by Susan Larsen

Illustrated by Beth Gabrielsen Williams

AuthorHouse™
1663 Liberty Drive
Bloomington, IN 47403
www.authorhouse.com
Phone: 833-262-8899

ISBN: 978-1-4343-3825-9 (sc)

Print information available on the last page.

Published by AuthorHouse 02/09/2021

authorHOUSE®

Dedicated to AnnElise and Nathan, Gifts from God, and Recipients of many Mommy Kisses

A special thank you to my husband, Marty, who encouraged me to put this story in print. I never would have done this without you. I love you!

Dedicated to my miracle babies, Caleb and Kiersten. You are my kisses from God.

To my Treasure, Page: Thank you for your honesty, support and encouragement. I love you!

One day a new baby girl was born. Her Mommy and Daddy loved her very much. They would kiss the little girl often.

However, when she became two years old she started "wiping the kisses off". At first the Mommy was sad. Then she started saying to her daughter,

"You can't wipe off Mommy kisses! They go in too fast and too deep!" She then added, "Some day you will need a Mommy kiss and I won't be there. Then you can reach inside and pull one out and know that I love you."

A little boy was born to the family. Around the age of two he also started trying to wipe off the Mommy kisses. So the Mommy started telling the son the same thing,

"You can't wipe off Mommy kisses. They go in too fast and too deep. Some day you will need a Mommy kiss and I won't be there. Then you can reach inside and pull one out and know that I love you."

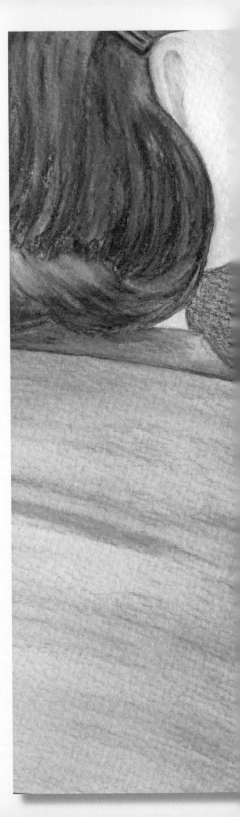

When the girl and boy grew up to be teenagers, the Mommy would walk into their rooms while they were asleep and tell them about Mommy kisses. Then she would blow them a kiss, whisper a prayer and go to bed.

One day after both of the children had finished school and were living on their own, the Mommy got a phone call from her son. He said, "Mom, do you remember all those Mommy kisses you used to give me?

Well, today I needed one and I reached inside and pulled one out. Thank you, Mom."

The Mommy cried.

A few years later the daughter had a daughter
of her own who had turned two years old.
One day the Mommy got a phone call. Her
daughter told her something that had just
happened at the store. She had given
her daughter a kiss and it got "wiped off."
Suddenly out of the daughter's mouth came
the same words she had heard many times
during her growing up years—

"You can't wipe off Mommy kisses, they go
in too fast and too deep. Some day you will
need a Mommy kiss and I won't be there. Then
you can reach inside and pull one out and
know that I love you."

Now the grandmother tries to kiss the grandchildren and sometimes the kisses are "wiped off". She tells them, "You can't wipe off Grammie kisses, they go in too fast and too deep. Some day you will need a Grammie kiss, and I won't be there. Then you can reach inside and pull one out and know that I love you."

The Grandmother figured that if Mommy kisses were good, Grammie kisses should be excellent!!

And so the story goes on
and on and on...

Someday perhaps you will
be able to give Mommy
kisses, or Grammie kisses,
or Auntie kisses. Always
remember that they go in
very fast and very deep
and are always there
inside when they are
needed. We adults need
them too... and they never
expire or run out.

We, Susan and Beth, have both been touched by God in incredible ways. Through life-threatening situations God has delivered us both. It was during those times that we felt not only kissed, but carried by God. In addition to being there in the midst of crises, He has walked with us through the drudgery, joy, and laughter of our daily lives.

This book is about a mother's kisses, but God gives the ultimate kisses that can't be rubbed off. Sometimes we try. But He reminds us to "reach inside and pull one out". How do you do this? By remembering that you have been kissed by Someone (Jesus) who loves you more than you could ever know; He demonstrated that love by dying on the cross for you in order to bring you to God! What an amazing 'kiss' that was and is!

If you would like to know how to experience that 'kiss' by God may we suggest you begin by reading the book of John in the New Testament of the Bible. God Bless You!

Printed in the United States
By Bookmasters